D1713469

Also by Elizabeth Arnold

LIFE

EFFACEMENT

CIVILIZATION

THE REEF

Skeleton Coast

Elizabeth Arnold

Skeleton Coast

FLOOD EDITIONS

Published by Flood Editions

www.floodeditions.com

ISBN 978-0-9903407-9-9

Design and composition by Quemadura

Cover photograph: Amy Schoeman,
*Aerial of Barchan Dunes North of
Lüderitz, Namibia.* Courtesy of the artist.

Printed on acid-free, recycled paper
in the United States of America

To Lindsay Bernal and Lisa McCullough

Yet take thy way; for sure thy way is best:
Stretch or contract me thy poor debtor:
This is but tuning of my breast,
    To make the music better.

GEORGE HERBERT

Skeleton Coast

ARC

I was
out of time before I started,

the Meyer lemon
blooming while full of fruit, our breezeway letting

a breeze through, its floor
smooth, that kind that stays cool

even in the worst north Florida heat,
so much of what we

don't understand and I
was out I was

out of time, the lemons
rotting, Marcus Aurelius, while you

sat on your bronze horse
in one of the highest squares of Rome, the metal

cold, a replica
probably

—you weren't Greek
nor was the original of your

statue (for once)
but I read you wrote your masterpiece,

calling it
not *Meditations* but

To Myself,
in Greek, the language of first minds

as yours was, is
and out of time, you

riding and riding through the cold north on an
endless-seeming

string of campaigns,
all through the north and the east

until you caught some
foreign illness

or other
again and this time

died of it.

DIURNAL

I had a dream
over and over as a child

in my

shimmering morning-light room,
    it was

set there, where I slept,

woodpeckers hammering at the eaves,
the river's waves' light

moving as if forever on the

far wall.
I'd wake (still asleep) in the dream

—I couldn't speak!—

as the two hands hovered.
So that even if I *thought* I'd say . . .

(if only to ask—

),
one would, white-gloved, hit

my face (I'd say

slapped but
the glove ate sound).

I don't remember waking.

CALF

The calf was tired from being born.
Its mother had disappeared.

Lying in the grass the bright brown

body with its
perfectly white face

as if deflating

thinned out of sight almost.
It could stand no longer

even with human help.

I thought it
lost.

But just a little later,

once the knowledgeable farmer
who runs the place arrived,

the mother was returned

and the calf played
skipping through the dimming light

of its first day.

0.016 SEC.

into the Trinity explosion
it looks like rock,

solid as clouds look from the ground

but smoother, a couple of specks
—birthmarks.

I guess this was a kind of birth,

or a little before—
the surface shiny in one photo

as if the light were expanding within a stretching birth sac

inside the mother
—quieter

than explosions usually are though

in this photo, still, the way the clouds of smoke
racing along the next ridge look from here,

—as clouds look from the ground

as I was saying,
these going sideways,

the angle of the smoke says so, fire roaring

underneath
—that's how they're made,

this kind of cloud

though you can't see the reality of it,
everything silent from where I'm standing, everything

stopped, stuck

just a few miles away across the valley,
a slight breeze rising,

cooling the air.
                Oppen said,

thinking of Vietnam:
A plume of smoke, visible at a distance

in which people burn.

EVERY NIGHT AT DINNER

I was the youngest, the only one left,
the arrangement of hydrangeas in the middle of the table

hiding us almost completely from each other,
light from the river shooting in.

What did he say to drive you back
into the kitchen every night

after having eaten precisely nothing?
You told me once that this was nothing

to worry about
but it happened all through high school every night

drawing a line between us in the
bright light sharp as a knife.

CATBIRD

A woody sprig of berries the catbird
crammed into her chick's mouth

but that fell three times off the high branch they were

perched on with the
mother bird

dutifully descending to the ground

to grab it, bring it back up
until

wide-eyed, fuzzy in its first feathers

(it hardly had a tail),
trying so hard to please and mostly failing,

the little one managed the inevitable act

of swallowing
what was offered

though the gift was nearly bigger than its head

which it shook a little before flying
following the mother anyway meowing.

ENCROACHMENT

The male is the aggressor
even in a birdbath full of sparrows,

mounting, determining what, when, going after

all that shouldn't be his
more than another's.

The only way for a woman to be

truly free
is to live alone, liberation

just too high a hurtle

with the man there, history being
a pile of tree trunks on our donkey backs.

GROWING UP IN THE SOUTH

I pulled my short white
socks up,

the kind I hated

to wear and then she'd haul me
over, folded them the right way,

the lace on the outside.

It was as if I'd
hurt her, my hands

hampered by the wrist-length gloves I'd put on

earlier, each finger
all the way in.

I didn't choose them any more than I

chose my mother or father
or the church

we were about to visit,

the crinoline crinkling loudly under my Sunday dress
as I climbed into the car.

I didn't buy

any of it, couldn't
own it. But I did live

and move by way of these things.

II

PERSON

His eyes were dead
the way sharks' seem to humans,

mine stunned

temporarily at least,
impermeable as marbles

—my eyes become his eyes.

I wish I'd heard
sooner

what he was in his voice,

the sounding through the mask made out of
bones and tendons,

various materials on stage

in ancient times, the voice vibrating
through that

singular as a fingerprint,

a person, personality
—one's

nature, stamp,

soul if you have one—
but maybe also who you'd like to think you are.

For him this was occurring

so it
wasn't all strategy

but partly, maybe essentially, a need

to be what he
wasn't, and to make

everybody else believe that.

I CAME UP AGAINST IT

madness.

It looked all right,
ordered even.

I went with it awhile. Then
"awhile" got
split up

hyphens everywhere glass

splintered trying to flow
instead of

stab without a will

so that there
couldn't have been

wouldn't
be
ever

a thing sustained—no single

moment
holding, stretching with
the skin intact

—just the
sharp shards' glint.

The man is hardly human.

WRECK

The drunk driver's wig fell off
then flew through the inside of her car

as she crossed mere paint and

slammed head-on into our car which,
once it stopped, smoked.

We're as lost as when we're

trying to tell the truth of what you say
or see past death:

you couldn't move your leg to get out.

I sat on the curb not helping
thinking I was bleeding down my back.

MY FRIEND STOOD
BEFORE HIM

screaming at his face
that he was

bad, a bad man.

Drunk, leaning over him
she yelled.

But he just

sank
a little deeper

in his leather chair,

smiled,
eyes glittering.

To be called on

for his crimes by her
—though nothing

he might

be called on for
ever could be

(by design

I see now)
punishable by the state—

turned him on.

DOUBT

I keep remembering things he said
I only half believed at the time

without acknowledging my doubt because I
didn't want what I perceived as

love I clung to stumbling falling
over almost
                to end.

GASLIGHTING

A word used to describe
an attempt to destroy another

's perception of reality.

Parents can gaslight children. Sociopaths
typically are very charming

and convincing liars

who deny wrongdoing
causing their victims

not only to doubt their own perceptions

but to assimilate what others project
onto them.

Hilde Lindemann argues

that in the case of women in particular
the victim's ability

to resist manipulation

depends on whether she can
trust her judgments

and that creating counterstories may help her

reacquire
an ordinary level of agency.

I SAW IT IN HER
EYES, HER GRIEF

she carries around unknowingly,
whole worlds storming

blue-black swirling

glimmering
in the stiffened face

like a fault deep in the ground

with its
inexact though statistically measurable need

to relieve stress over time

without the slightest care for
what else might go.

IN UPPER EGYPT

I scratched his name and number out
with the intensity of the early Copts

chiseling at the heads of former gods.

EXPOSED

He walked up to the photo that took
hours to expose

—by moonlight!—the tall thin bottle at the center

a cold white, half shadows brushed against
the deep black ground behind it.

There's a

stillness it holds.
There was the blankness in his face as he stood there,

eyes unblinking as a god's,

indicative (in this realm) of the gap
in the orbital cortex

of the sociopath,

right above the eyes in the brain scan—
appearing dead white

—*no*:

black. So
the pupil grows to meet that

and it swallows her.

ETYMOLOGIES

Live ... A.S. libban ... orig. to remain, be left behind.
Deceive ... L. dēcipere, to take away.

WALTER SKEAT

You took my life

as I knew it.
I was

gone, couldn't work, think,

though I only learned what really happened
a whole year later

—there was a strategy,

to see I had to
be told, the experience otherwise

nameless, without form.

At the time anyway
that it was happening.

Remains, though—*that* me—

I was
remaindered.

I wouldn't call it living.

HE

comforted me,
my being at home with being misled

by those who mislead themselves sometimes

as we all do,
pulled toward something

true

or not
partly because

we can't get hold of what's going on

in the other's mind
when all that's craved

is someone to rely on.
                              But I

don't, can't, want
only what's

familiar but also

seemingly (it must be!) real,
the ground forever moving out from under me,

my having emerged

inside that kind of motion,
love there unconvincingly convincing

—what I

though still seek,
these things I know from childhood, remembering

inaccurately clearly because I'm

thinking of
safety in that context.

Safety!
            There's a

warmth though,
in the odors, how

the wind feels off the river.

LOVE

To look past one's desire can be
a withering thing

like when I heard you lie in court

about what happened
—I was there! Just as the

house finch is to be distinguished

from the purple.
You have to

look without a heart to see.

ELEGY OF THE SELF

I heard my heart again
not beating like a drum but

shimmying

like an old jazz drummer
tired, playing in a trio in a bar with velvety

maroon wallpaper peeling in a bombed-out part of town

brushing his airy brush across the surface
of the snare, making

gestures more than beats that way

like the marks a piece of chalk pulled across a blackboard on its side makes
or the fuzzy look of a comet—no

backbone there

evidently, nothing to
hold a being up.
                    I give my

everything away, you take it.

HELL

Imagine falling into a well
with plenty of water in it,

maybe some

maidenhair fern
feathering in arcs out from the walls

like the one I looked down in St. Augustine,

the vertical round of stone
straight, smooth

and nobody sees you

fall or hears—I have to tread water
for how long?

     *

The abuse continued three years
—even into his time at college.

"I don't know why I let it go on for so long.
I've been asking myself that for decades."

                *

Kohut says the narcissist requires
total control of his environment

including the desire

for revenge, for
righting a wrong,

in an attempt to turn from

passive victimization
to the active role of giving pain to others.

                *

He needs her,
she the dead one,

shrine of blurry photos on the

laptop I lent him
where she looks

permanently saddened,

fake fiancé who can't
talk back now, age, show him

who he is

—but that would only be,
after all, for him, to be

a one who's feigning what we'd

all hoped too readily
again and again·

that in his

bait, his body,
is a soul.

     *

Great circulatory movements of Earth,
the ocean's rivers and

streams of air

jerked from their beds,
those hollows we imagine, runnels

that aren't there!

—the air thus free to
fluctuate, test boundaries. Just as the

Berbers living in Siwa

at the western edge of Egypt
simply wander across the border to Libya

—it's a pretty barren place,

the Great Sand Sea of the Sahara—
and the weakening

jet stream flowing over Canada,

the warm Gulf Stream to the right
protecting Europe, and

the freezing Benguela Current farther south

just west of southern Africa
that moderates that portion of that continent's air,

veneration never follows age,

not these days,
the material aspect disappearing

into another material aspect.

*

Kunlangeta is Yupik
for a man who repeatedly

lies and cheats and

steals things,
takes advantage of women,

who doesn't pay attention to reprimands

and who's always being brought
to the elders for punishment

What to

do with such a person?
When no one's looking

push him, she said, right off the ice shelf.

*

I think not getting straight talk
from the beginning

teaches a person, oddly,

to believe more readily in others
maybe because the person

craves that a little more

and a lack of
follow-up questioning of the

vague answers

you *are* getting to your
(amazingly!)

even vaguer questions

fearing learning something leading you
out of there goddammit.

    *

In the performance of the *Oresteia*
I saw at Court Theatre in Chicago

the furies spoke by way of

not just words but the
grayish purple pocket-like leotards they wore

—not tight-fitting but tight enough that

moment to moment you'd see
an elbow maybe, a head

(no face),

a nose, knee, then
a head again at some new angle

while the actors undulated as they sang

Aeschylus's thick words
out of the earth

where Athena's light even couldn't shine.

She had to lift them
out of there

into the world of reason.

They submitted
but I never really bought that.

    *

A blank came into my life. A negative.
I lay with him night after night.

*

In a documentary
filmed off the coast of Cape Town,

sardines school

making an elusive column
called a bait ball

constantly moving, swirling

so as to seem to be a single, larger thing
and solid,

fooling predators.

*

What to do to make my winters
bearable. The backyard in spring

—where *is* it?

*

The Maya believe in a
cyclical nature of life—nothing is ever

born and nothing dies.

Beneath the earth is the dark realm
out of which grows

the Tree of Life

coming up through the earth
towering into the heavens

through thirteen levels

to reach paradise.
One doesn't die and go to a heaven

or a hell but rather

embarks on a journey
beginning in the dark

and treacherous underworld

where the inhabitants
are more apt to

trick and destroy a soul than help one.

*

It's as simple as this: in practice,
if you go and make a call in tennis,

make it with confidence,

I tell her. Because sometimes she's
not so sure and gives it away.

It's not that you're being nice.

You're sending the signal to the other
player that they're able to

come and enter your territory.

     *

Kohut says
the very structure of the self

is enfeebled so
rage can't flower into real

assertiveness
leading to oversensitivity and

more rage.

*

I'm hard to get to know
she said. It's

funny because

from my end everything's streaming endlessly forward toward the other
but I wonder now because I

trust her

intelligence, her fairness
—there's got to be something to what she's saying:

when talking to another on and on

my words are
bricks in a wall apparently.

*

I'm here, I said, because there's no
refuge, finally, from myself.

*

How thrilling to look
into clear water off the coast

of a rocky island in the tropics, see through what

cannot so often be seen through
—usually it's murky—

like a face hiding the mind.

IV

SICK BIRDS

don't show it, live a little longer as
looking the least bit vulnerable leads

to their destruction

before they've had the chance to
die from the inside.

Faking health

frees them to fall in their own time,
throw up a little dust.

I LOOK INTO HIS EYES

What do I see? What I
think only?

Even when feeling deeply I'm not

reliably knowing, seeing.
A friend said

You lack self-regard.

I wish too much
to please sometimes

which doesn't make me good

as I was taught to think growing up.
It's not hopeful, the

ego watery.

A lack that has the force to floor me in midlife.
But like the ana trees

growing in riverbeds in Namibia

when the thirty-year flood comes
roaring through,

somehow after all this

I'm still standing.
It's hard to know why.

I've lost meaning.

Like everybody else I'm hardly more than
one shot or heart collapse from leaving.

No one will care, not really.

We say we will but
we go on, get over

whatever it is that's happened,

a loss, losses,
so easily,

go mad if we have to.

I'M BEGINNING TO SEE

Though clearly strategic in his acts
against me

—and his mother

and all the other women who came before,
and whomever he's with now,

using—

I see he needs the lies
for a sense of

self, so what he pulled over on me

he's pulling over on himself
—he needs that,

to fill in

what's lacking,
a story, history.

It's not so much a crime, then, as

an emotional requirement. The life he's imagined
for himself he

keeps repeating with each victim

to continue the dream,
believe.

When he panics, becomes enraged,

rabid dog because he fears
the story could be exposed,

it's this invisible survival that's on the line, his

self, whole being,
spine

—why the lies rang true, fool.

WEATHER RADAR

In the black-and-white satellite image
like photos astronauts took of the moon (except

there wasn't any weather there)

as the mostly tinfoil orbiter descended
toward the surface

so slowly that first time

while everybody watched in awe
or as in an X-ray,

you can see how far the hurricane reaches

beyond its eye,
the cloud-cover crinkling

as of the finest cloth

or plastic wrap
snagged

going so far past even the outer bands of the storm's huge body

swirling, the clouds as if whipped:
everything's involved

as with a scar across the back, the numbness extending

farther than you'd thought possible—to the
leg maybe, or the other

foot—

there being a feeling of being
pulled, a little bit of

pain, or a lot,

but usually it's a tugging almost imperceptibly at what should be the
virgin shape of a shape

of the original body, a (in this context)

perfect form
emerging in the womb

as how a mind scarred by an unkind act

smaller than you'd think
could produce a result that great

or that enduring.

SO MAYBE I'M RIGHT TO THINK

he was a victim
—from way back in his life, I mean;

his father abused his

mother, maybe him too,
but even if he didn't get regularly hit,

to have experienced the mother's pain

while a child
could have sent

something in him up as a wall.

I was furious,
not the kind of water that can be looked into

at that time, too much

particulate matter,
stain of the oak leaves,

too much oxygen stirred up at the surface.

But now it's a little more settled
here at the house.

There's not much light but I'm starting to see

farther—see what's *here*.
Wherever it is I am.

HAWKS

Hawks kettling on the thermals
high above the Appalachians on their way south—it looks like

thought, the mind floating by way of association, veering

and floating, circling back
to the impinging weight of a remembered event

or nonevent of—as what led here in the first place—

mind, the movement of the mind
outweighing any material force or falling

which is the origin of force

—where there's gravity that is—a falling toward
what ultimately no one knows of,

human thinking reaching

just so far
past what can be seen

by way of scientific instruments

such as solar wind out of the sun's atmosphere
then into Earth's

appearing in the form

of changes in the weather or a loss of electrical power
—thus entering

a house, a room, the space freeing the mind

without the intimidation of those stands of pines reflected in
Greek groves of columns,

the catalpa's imposing plate-sized leaves.

SKELETON COAST

I

Here, there's nothing more than the evidence of water
though under the dry bed of the Hoanib

and all the other rivers branching through

the far northwest of Namibia
the water's close enough to the surface for elephants to reach it

just by digging

with their enormous as if weighted feet
pawing at the sand

even though the river flows

only once every thirty years,
can't make it to the sea.

And the furies stream into my subterrane

galloping along the hidden veins
snorting loud as the rare mountain zebras I saw

a few miles in from Skeleton Coast.

We had to drive off-road
to find them,

over boulders,

sudden uneven drops,
the truck leaning close to tipping.

It was a family group: two females, one foal,

and the stallion
with its muscled haunches.

They were so well camouflaged, bright, the colors of the land

intensifying as we moved east,
very little green there generally

—except in the flood plain I call Eden,

a large low place, lush,
where the few animals that can survive

life in a desert

gather to graze and become prey in
—then suddenly

these reds and purples,

deep orange
and a brown that's almost black.

The zebras have flat-bottomed hooves

for running up into the hills from danger I was told.
But why run? They match the land so well

you look right through them.

II

On the other side of the mind
's experience,

above subconscious happenings such as fear,

too human in my turning away and
running from the mess

I haven't taken in apparently,

running laughing away
from everything underground—I'm

bifurcated clear through,

back to back my two halves shun each other
unaware of the split

or of the deeper calm interior,

silent,
waiting for me to stop

long enough to hear that, hope.

III

In fifty-seven years
I think I've only seen her face face me

—opening, offering
for me
                    for her too!—

twice.

IV

Why can't they
leave it in the ground, the oil, coal,

all that grief?

World, world of the
mind-destroying chant of the furies

that binds one's thinking,

sung to no lyre,
a song to shrivel men up!

V

It looked like the wall surrounding Rome,
tall, slightly curved along the Hoanib

as if it were made of tuff

but actually, here, what looks man-made is
packed sand, not stone,

a wall built by a river

holding over so much time,
for as long as Rome's, maybe longer—who knows?—

made by water running rarely and

not really all that hard
most of the time

but with a vengeance when the flood comes

in a torrent,
the power of that,

of water merely running cutting

land into so perfect an as-if-human-made wall over time.
Within a couple of days of the flood

everything's dust again, everything's beige,

a color that eats life,
death to the eye you know

and yet a pretty good number of animals thrive there.

VI

I say inside my mind

you've got to
trust yourself you're worth that

as the Earth (us)

must think
nothing from outside

ever will

maliciously or by accident
pass through the atmosphere

that's open wide and watery as an eye.

VII

Look: there's a go-away bird
fighting with a hawk to save her eggs.

Go-away, go-away, she says.

VIII

Out at the coast, ship carcasses teeter
or sand-heavy at their centers, sunk,

buckle,
all that's left being rusted bones, the little bit of tackle still attached

like wiry hairs,

the bones of their past occupants
bright against the dun of the dunes—nothing

for a survivor to survive on

after the fogs hid the shoreline
from the ships,

nothing but dunes of a mind-boggling variety of shapes

—all just sand
finally, lions hunting among them

and the tiny plants waiting for morning

when the fog will grant them water of a measure
smaller than drops

as the deep dunes multiply inland hundreds of miles before

anyone could reach
the green of Etosha's famous watering hole

or one of the few minute ponds
scattered around

no doubt no one found.

IX

It was you!
—or a version of you,

a you with you inside him

so far south of Skeleton Coast
and something like ten very large countries

south of where you live, the sand there

unlike Aswan's
every shade of red

from blood-orange to lipstick-pink.

I saw you, no mistake,
the skin the same, bulk, same laugh, eye,

voice,

all of the what-
of-the-first-you-you-I-still-love

even after so much time.

When I left Sossusvlei I left you, or this you, this
avatar, intact,

didn't touch him, give him any trouble,

not even with my voice
or if so only a little

but it wasn't the kind of sound that held us in its hum,

the you yours harmonizing
more and more with the mine-mine,

a cave made out of that.

TWO RIVERS

after Lawrence Langer

When the woman facing the video camera speaks
decades after having been freed

from whichever death camp she'd been dumped in

about how life is for her now,
it's clear she was never freed, not really,

two rivers running through her,

one roaring, drowning out the other
which nevertheless keeps going

barely preserving

societal norms, those
kindnesses, considerations,

thinking of others, the future of the state.

But the louder river's stronger. It erodes its bed,
pulls like a muscled eel against the line

because she couldn't turn her back on what she'd had to do to

not die, the slightest seam left in the water
for so short a time!—like a breath.

Me? I'd have sunk

so readily into the murk
as into one who'd have killed me for a dime. And I did

sink, gave

everything for nothing.
                                  Why can't I say

what it hurts to know about the self?

—while she can't *not*
say it, staring straight into the eye of the lens:

"Love leaves me cold."

BIRDS NEAR THE COAST

of the Yucatán Peninsula
zip by fast as flies, a sooty-looking small one

taking a short cut through the jungle

past the cinnamon-coated coati lumbering down
the slow-motion twisting elastic trunk

of a ficus as an ibis arcs

low over mangrove scrub out
near the water,

the airy roots reaching from the middle branches

straight for the earth.
They don't waste time on the wrong person.

SOURCE

By the time we'd turned our horses
back toward home

shifting to a gallop once the downpour started

that threatened to soak the white sand road,
at first the raindrops merely slid

over and down the dry slopes

and collapsing ruts
the horses' hooves sank into

half disappearing

as I tried to explain whatever it was I needed
so desperately for you to hear,

yelled as the rain got harder.

But you kept looking straight ahead
as if you were deaf, no hope for a flow between us,

each word with its pool of meanings

existing only for the speaker,
words as material as rain

torpedoing sand instead of being

springs, *sources*
of imagination, love—of civilization.

KNOWING

The pass thrown
where the wide receiver isn't,

thrown at

air, a gap time leaves.
It's a

backwards leaving,

future-to-past
or forward to the future you might say,

taking skill

—and faith I've learned—
to aim at a space like that

knowing it will fill.

DESERT

Just across the border from north Texas

my car broke, the land's heat
hovered above the defunct road

I'd rolled it onto

with a clump of empty, yellowish buildings
at the dead end,

the exit on the interstate being

there I guess
only for the road that actually

goes somewhere

in the opposite direction,
its border as deserted as my part

until the eye caught

dust-colored cardboard-box-like houses
lining the red hill's foot

far south across

the roar of highway.
The car was dead, useless

—no way away

from this place so I sat in the heat
with the windows up

for as long as I could stand it—and my

dog—waiting for the tow truck,
then rolled them down

a little, just a crack because I

feared some slasher-movie kind of incident,
cruelty that seemed

fitting here,

the sun being cruel
and the sharp sand grains—then

more, rolled the windows

farther down, then all the way but even
that wasn't enough, so I

opened the door

as if it had been years that I'd been
in there,

broke a seal, as if it had been

millennia
since someone,

some kind of mason probably,

with the hope and fear of anarchic times,
had walled me in

to preserve

      —what for what?
As if a living thing could leave its tomb.

I ended up on the car hood

where these birds I didn't recognize
fed on locusts

it looked like. There was the

click of exoskeletons,
a remarkable display of leaping

—by the birds! (it wasn't flying)—as they

went by turns into the cloud, came out
invariably with a bug in the beak,

then shot back in,

my dog tugging at the leash
but we were

free, me barely catching breath in

wonderment
at another kind of what.

QUINTANA ROO

The current took us boatless through
the spindly daddy-longleg-like white trunks of the mangroves,

the creek water filled with light

all the way down to the sandstone
covered with a film of

slightly less-white mud,

floor of the thousands-year-old Maya waterway
linking two lagoons.

We were a little group of strangers passing

though one of us I'd traveled parallel to
for more than twenty years

wandering, weaving in and out of the same flow, rivers in a river.

We'd parted for the last time finally
except for this last silent trip

down a creek—the silence loud!—with the others.

But also not with
as it always really is for all of us

alone or not at the same time

or alternately and often
even when the tie with the other is stronger

than it is now.

At last I knew, saw
as I floated in a new stillness,

the water clear as air

under and all around me
as if bodiless, a soul in timeless space

with a surprising balance in the water on my own

when a green heron,
female (brown), hopped

barely visible branch to branch

through the looping branches or roots of a mangrove
—soon to become roots anyway as they

reached tentatively

but also
casually, carelessly toward the ground:

The only way out is through.

Notes and Acknowledgments

p. 10: The lines quoted at the end of the poem are from George Oppen's "Of Being Numerous."

p. 27: The verb "gaslight" comes from the 1938 play, *Gas Light*, by Patrick Hamilton, in which a scheming husband persistently denies the reality of his wife's perceptions in an attempt to degrade her identity and drive her mad. In *Damaged Identities, Narrative Repair*, the philosopher Hilde Lindemann theorizes about how gaslighting affects women. The poem uses words and phrases from and regarding Lindemann's writings.

p. 31: The photograph referred to here is by Jay Shoot.

In "Hell," at various points I use words and phrases from these sources:

    p. 41: Amos Kamil's reporting on the sex scandal at the Horace Mann School, first published in the *New York Times Magazine*, June 6, 2012;

    p. 42: Heinz Kohut's writing on narcissistic personality disorder;

    p. 45: anthropologist Jane M. Murphy's discovery of *kunlangeta*, a Yupik word meaning "the man without moral feeling," "the unscrupulous man," "his mind knows what to do but he does not do it," used by an isolated group of Yupik-speaking Inuits living near the Bering Strait (*Science*, March 1976);

    p. 48: a discussion of Maya religious beliefs in Joshua J. Mark's entry for "Maya Culture" (6 July 2012) from the online *Ancient History Encyclopedia*;

    p. 50: what tennis coach Rob Steckley told Lucie Safarova;

    p. 51: a poster hung in the rehab wing of the Western New Mexico Correctional Facility 70 miles west of Albuquerque, New Mexico, where Dr. Kent Kiehl did scans on the brains of inmates for two studies, one about drug abuse and one about sociopathy (John Seabrook, "Suffering Souls: The Search for the Roots of Psychopathy," *The New Yorker*, 10 November 2008).

p. 71: Here I use words spoken by the furies in Aeschylus's *Oresteia.*

Versions of poems in this collection appeared in *American Literary Review, Chicago Review, Eco-Theo, Los Angeles Book Review, The Nation,* and *Ploughshares.*

I wish to thank the MacDowell Colony, where I drafted many of these poems over a two-month period, and the University of Maryland's College of the Arts and Humanities for their generous support. And last but not least, many many thanks to Devin and Michael at Flood.